THE RHYMES AND TIMES OF LIFE

THE RHYMES AND TIMES OF LIFE

Alan Hatcher

ARTHUR H. STOCKWELL LTD
Torrs Park   Ilfracombe   Devon
Established 1898
www.ahstockwell.co.uk

© *Alan Hatcher, 2011*
First published in Great Britain, 2011
All rights reserved.
*No part of this publication may be reproduced
or transmitted in any form or by any means,
electronic or mechanical, including photocopy,
recording, or any information storage and
retrieval system, without permission
in writing from the copyright holder.*

*British Library Cataloguing-in-Publication Data.
A catalogue record for this book is available
from the British Library.*

ISBN 978-0-7223-4087-5
*Printed in Great Britain by
Arthur H. Stockwell Ltd
Torrs Park   Ilfracombe
Devon*

CONTENTS

Eyes Looking at You	7
Furniture Move	8
No Ambition	10
Moaner	11
One to Carry	12
What a Pong!	13
The Diet	14
What a Snore!	15
DIY?	16
Nuisance Calls	17
Sit Down	18
Seagulls	19
Trampoline	20
A Slight Exaggeration	21
Veggie Diet	22
Foot Trouble	23
Sunday Lunch	24
Childhood	26
Shaving Time	27
The Shed	28
Spring	30
Mirror, Mirror	31
Not Good Enough	32
Little Children	34
Mother and Daughter	35
Cheeky!	36
Mum	37
The Interview	38
Flies	40
False Teeth	41
Snobs?	42
Bump Start	44
Fred	45
Don't Eat Between Meals	46
Auntie Dot	47

We Need a Rota	48
Dressing Up	49
Handbags and Shoes	50
Our Anniversary	52
My New Wellies	53
The Open Fire	54
Bad Habits	55
The Best Man's Speech	56
Diesel	58
Too Much Information	60
Shadows	62
Big-Head	63

EYES LOOKING AT YOU

I was reading the paper and heard a yell,
I was quite shocked and thought, 'What the hell!'
It was the wife making that awful din.
I rushed to the bathroom, rushed right in.
"Get it out!" was the awful shout,
Then I saw what the fuss was about.
Well, I'm sorry – I just had to laugh,
Because it sat there right in the bath.
Just a spider, there it sat,
Hairy legs, long, big and fat.
To me it looked quite harmless sitting there,
But to tell my wife that, I didn't dare.
"It won't hurt you," I had to say.
"Get it out and throw it away!
Those big beady eyes keep looking at me.
I came in here – I just want a wee."
I caught the spider and put it outside,
And so my wife was pacified.
But it makes me wonder why spiders choose
To invade and frequent bathrooms and loos.

FURNITURE MOVE

We man the phone and do our best
To be polite and answer each request.
A typical question this could be:
"Have you got a spare desk for me?"
Or "I would like, if you have it,
A nice four-drawer filing cabinet."
We move and deliver furniture constantly –
That's all part of our job, you see –
Moving desks and cupboards too.
In our time we've moved quite a few,
But last week was a quiet week.
No one seemed to want to speak.
Then I found out where and when
Furniture was on the move again.
There were beds and chairs to shift.
Good job we have an electric lift!
We moved all the beds today;
It was chairs and tables yesterday.
With the help of some of the nurses,
A bit of moaning and a few curses,
At least we achieved our aim.
But perhaps we'll have to move it back again.
When moving things we always get advice.
I've heard it said more than once or twice;
"Watch your back!" is the usual cry,
But I can't, no matter how hard I try.
I don't have eyes in the back of my head;
I was born with them in front instead.

So, satisfied with a good job done,
I said goodbye and thanked everyone.
So home I go and, to my relief,
I'll have a sit and rest – that's my belief.
I get home and, to top the lot,
The wife has done a furniture-swap.
I looked aghast because I found
She had moved it all right round.
But she said to me, "I don't like that.
Do you think you could move it all right back?"
"Yes, my dear," I said quite meekly.
"That's what I do – I do it weekly."

NO AMBITION

I often think of long ago and of my special dreams,
But I'm afraid life has passed me by, or so it seems.
I guess I'm Mr Ordinary, lacking in ambition –
I couldn't even win a prize in any exhibition.
I could have been a pop star if I could only sing,
But a pop star without a voice wouldn't mean a thing.
Maybe I could have been a footballer in my younger day,
But it's no good even trying if it's a game you cannot play.
What about an artist? I could be good at that,
Except when I painted pictures they looked rather flat.
One can only imagine, one can only dream,
And think of things long ago and things that might have been.

MOANER

As I drive to work and leave from home,
I stop at traffic lights and I groan.
I mutter under my breath and say,
"Those damn lights weren't there yesterday."
There's no one there to agree with me,
But I carry on whinging constantly.
There's nothing like a good old moan,
And, I'm pleased to say, I'm not on my own.
When you walk down any street –
Doesn't matter whom you meet –
Weather is the topic of conversation.
We're obsessed with it – the whole damn nation.
We moan about if there's too much rain.
Two weeks' hot weather, it's just the same.
We go on about the youngsters and often say,
"Things weren't like that in our younger day."
Of course they weren't, and in our hearts
We know that we're a load of moaning old farts.
The other day we went to the shops,
Thought we would buy some nice pork chops.
When I moaned about the price of meat,
The butcher would not admit defeat.
He grinned and said, "My suggestion is
Try our delicious pork sausages."
I could go on and on constantly,
But I know there's people worse off than me.

ONE TO CARRY

All through life I've tried to care,
And as for work, I've done my share.
But do you find, just like me,
There's always one to carry, constantly?
Every team has one, I do declare,
But it doesn't really seem quite fair.
There's those that are always late for work
And treat it as a special perk.
If things go wrong, they blame the tool,
But still they make out they do it all.
It should not come as a real surprise,
They're the ones always on about a rise.
Let me tell you about this bloke I knew
Who didn't want too much to do.
If memory serves me right, as I recall,
He never really did much at all.
I don't know why they gave him a job –
He was a bone-idle, lazy slob.
When there was extra work to do,
He would manage to sneak to the loo.
Lunchtimes he would sit and doze,
Mouth and eyes half open, semi-comatose.
I gave the table a mighty thump –
Cor, you ought to have seen him jump!
I've never seen him move so fast.
It gave all the rest of us quite a laugh.

WHAT A PONG!

Out of my bed and rise at dawn,
Window flung open and curtains drawn.
My wife exclaims, "What the hell!
Is that you that made that awful smell?"
I must admit it was quite strong,
It smelt sickly rich – a rotten pong.
We got in the car, out for the day,
Just to really get away.
And as we got just down the lane,
We came across that rotten smell again.
And as I thought – what I was dreading –
The farmer was out, manure-spreading.
I ranted and raved and raised my fist.
The farmer came over – he looked quite miffed.
"This is the country and, as you know,
I must spread manure to make things grow."
"Yes," I said, "but chicken manure reeks."
"Don't worry, mate – it only lasts for weeks."
Not amused by his silly joke,
I started to cough, and nearly choke.
Holding my breath, and temper too,
I said, "I'm not going to win this debate with you."
Back in the car and on our way,
There is only one more thing to say.
That awful smell, I must admit,
I really don't like to smell of it.

THE DIET

I received a letter to summon me
To have a check-up by my GP.
So off I went bearing several thoughts,
Not quite too chipper, out of sorts.
He said to me, "As your doctor and a friend,
Here is what I thoroughly recommend –
This, my friend, is my advice to you:
You should lose at least a stone or two.
In actual fact, it should be more –
Perhaps it should be three or four.
Go and see the nurse. She's a dietician.
She's an expert on your condition."
So off I went. She was very nice –
She gave me lots of good advice.
"Cut out the chocolate and the sweets –
No ice cream, cakes, or other treats.
Cut out the spirits and the beer.
Cut down on alcohol. Do I make it clear?
Maybe a glass or two of wine at the weekend."
I'm sure this diet will drive me round the bend.
Fresh green salad – that's the stuff! –
But after five days of it I've had enough.
Too much red meat can be bad,
But two thin slices on a plate look sad.
The wife said to me, to my surprise,
"From now on, no more meat pies!
We'll cut down on spuds, rice and pasta too –
I'll go on a diet, just like you."
Eat five a day, that's what they say –
That'll help you shed those pounds away.
I thought I ate enough fruit before –
Now the house looks like a greengrocery store.
I've gone without and tried hard, but fear
I'm never going to be Slimmer of the Year.

WHAT A SNORE!

As I get home I cheerfully say,
"That's the end of another working day."
After dinner we sit and watch the news,
But my eyes feel heavy and I start to snooze.
As I drift away and I start to nod
I feel my ribs get a gentle prod.
"Wake up! You have started snoring."
"Sorry, dear, but I find the telly boring.
I don't think I really snore."
"You must be joking! You could be heard next door."
"I am really sure that I don't snore."
"You do – you did last night, and the night before."
I sit back and relax in the old armchair;
I soon drift off again, as if I don't care.
"You should go to bed, say goodnight to me –
You really are a hopeless case, not good company."

DIY?

I'll redesign your kitchen, just you wait and see.
We'll save a lot of money, just for you and me.
Just tell me what you really want,
And I'll have a real good go.
I'm very good at DIY, although a little slow.
Decorating the dining room is my latest project.
I'm sorry, dear, if it's taken all year and I'm still not finished yet,
The furniture is in the way and looks a bit untidy.
I promise to clear it up and have it done by Friday.
Now, getting back to this idea of mine,
Look at this magazine – look at the design.
The way you look at me, you don't look impressed.
I know I'm sitting down, but I need a little rest.
I think it's time to have a talk and review the situation.
If you're not satisfied, please accept my resignation.
I'll give up this DIY – I'll give it up for good.
I think it will give you peace of mind, and I know you think I should.

NUISANCE CALLS

Do you ever get nuisance calls
From people that take us for fools?
When you sit down to have a meal,
The phone rings. I know how you feel.
The other night it was just amazing –
Someone trying to sell me double glazing.
"It's cost effective" is what he said.
"Will the council pay?" The phone went dead.
Well now, just the other day,
This chap rang up just to say
He could save us money on fuel bills –
No complications and no frills.
"Sign a gas agreement from today."
"That's a laugh! We don't have gas anyway!"
Now, it's really strange but funny
How everybody wants to save me money.
Why is it in some stranger's view
That they know what's best for you.
They don't even take the hint when told
That my dinner's getting cold.
Cheaper mortgage and cheaper loans,
Cheaper insurance, even mobile phones!
I raise my voice to sound impressive,
But I'm feeling quite aggressive.
"I don't need any extra credit.
I won't repeat it – I've just said it."
They talk to me about the credit crunch,
But I'm just fed up with the telephone bunch.
Now on the phone I'm not too polite,
Especially when these idiots ring at night.
"Now I've had it – I've had enough –
So just clear off. Go and get stuffed!"

SIT DOWN

As I sit upon this seat
It hurts my rump – there's not much meat.
The other thing that I find:
I've got plenty in front, but not much behind.
The other thing with seats with slats:
They're bad for bums and bad for backs.
Stand and grow good, that's what they say,
But I can't stand up all day.
As I stand up from this slatted seat,
That looks so fine and looks so neat,
I find I've got a rough corrugated ass,
So I think I'll just get up and sit on the grass.

SEAGULLS

Summer days are long and hot;
Night-times I don't sleep a lot.
But when it's quiet, dark and still,
I can hear the seagulls shrill.
They shriek and call through the night.
It could give someone an awful fright.
You'd think that, screeching through the day,
They'd all be pleased to hide away.
Now, wouldn't it be quite bliss
If someone invented a seagull dish?
Seagull hotpot or seagull stew –
I think I might try it, wouldn't you?
I know they tend to make me cuss,
But I'm not really that serious.
I'm not proposing a seagull diet –
I just want some peace and quiet.
There's plenty of room for them at sea,
And seaside towns would for the better be –
No more mess or seagull muck!
But, as for now, no such luck.

TRAMPOLINE

On hot and sunny summer days
I like to sit out and laze.
I like to sit out in the shade,
Drinking ice-cold lemonade.
But peace and quiet is shattered, there's no doubt,
When the kids next door come out.
Why do they have to shout and scream
On that ruddy trampoline?
My wife says I shouldn't make a fuss,
But it makes me swear and cuss.
Lots of shouting, lots of noise –
Don't they have some quiet toys?
Then their mother's had enough,
Tells them off for playing rough,
Tells the kids to get inside –
That makes me smug and satisfied.

A SLIGHT EXAGGERATION

I expect you've heard some stories in your time,
But just you wait until you've heard mine.
Now, don't you laugh – it's not a joke –
I'd hate for you to cough and choke.
Now, there was this bloke that I once knew –
He could really spin a yarn or two.
Now, we all knew he was a liar
When he told us about the frying pan on the fire.
He told us about this old brave cat
That jumped in the pan and danced in hot fat.
There it was, dancing round and round,
Quite happily bolting eggs and bacon down.
Listening intently was this other guy.
He said, "I can top that story, and here's the reason why:
Yesterday morning, just looking out the window,
I saw the neighbour's cat sneaking up the spud row.
Right there and then he dug out a shallow pit,
Then he proceeded to leave a large deposit.
He then turned round and filled the hole he'd dug."
He said, "What do you think of that?" looking rather smug.
The first man said, "All cats do that, and you can't say they don't."
"Yeah, I know that, but not with a shovel they don't."
Now the moral of this story – and I hope you realise –
Is that there's nothing to be gained by the art of swapping lies.

VEGGIE DIET

I know that a mate of mine has tried to keep it very quiet,
But I know for sure that he's started a vegetarian diet.
His wife has chosen this plan of action to improve his health.
All I say is good luck to them! I don't fancy it myself.
They say it's very natural and they say it's good for you,
But after trying some of the recipes I'm not sure it's true.
Especially when it's cooking, I don't like the smell.
It gives me severe heartburn and gives me wind as well.
The other day I met my friend sitting in the pub.
He said he was fed up with his diet and fancied proper grub.
I suggested that with his pint he had a nice pork pie.
"No need to tell the wife," I said. "Just eat it on the sly."
He said he could not do that; he said it would be cheating;
He said that if he gave in to whims, it would be self-defeating.
Now I've nothing but admiration for all the veggie type,
But as for being that healthy, is it all a load of hype?
I can see that if I ate only vegetables I would be much thinner,
But I can't imagine no meat upon my plate when I have my dinner.
All vegetables are good for you – of that there's no denying –
But when served up with nice roast meat they're far more satisfying.
Now for breakfast in the morning it could be cereals or toast,
But for me it's eggs and bacon – it's what I like the most.
If I have veg-only meals, you'd better keep your distance,
Because I guarantee it doesn't agree with me; it gives me flatulence.
It's common knowledge that kids don't like veg –
It's something that they hate.
They will eat their meat first and push the veggies round the plate.
If you don't agree with me or you have a doubt,
Just you try to get any kid to eat a Brussels sprout.

FOOT TROUBLE

It seems long ago that I'd go walking up and down the street,
With brand-new suit, slim-jim tie, and new shoes upon my feet.
I'd ignore people that walked by, and all their laughs and snickers.
I didn't care that they'd stare because I had my winkle-pickers.
"How can you wear things like that? How can you wear those?
They must really hurt your feet and even pinch your toes."
Times and fashions seem to alter, and we had a brand-new phase:
Chisel-toe shoes were the in thing next. That was the latest craze.
I'd changed my job by now and worked on the roads for a living,
I wore leather steel-capped boots – they were completely unforgiving.
Sometimes I wore wellingtons that made my mates laugh.
They came so high up my thigh they nearly chafed my arse.
Wearing them home at night, by the door I'd take off one welly.
The wife said, "Don't bring them in – I think they're rather smelly."
She would stand by the door and glare, fingers holding her nose,
Still moaning and complaining, saying, "I don't like the smell of those,"
Waving her hand in front of her, saying things I can't repeat.
The gist of it was she couldn't stand the smell of cheesy feet.
"I'll get a tub of water and put in suds and soap.
You can sit by the fire and give your feet a good soak."
It was some time after labouring and, to my recollection,
I changed my job in life, in a completely new direction.
I've got a real posh job now. They provide us with a nice uniform.
They give us leather boots as well – I really must conform.
Oh no! I'm afraid to say, it's those boots with the steel toecaps.
I know it's for our own safety's sakes, to prevent any mishaps,
But they still make my feet ache and they make them sore.
They also make them stink and sweaty like they did before.
With my crooked toes, corns and calluses, I could make a list.
Perhaps I should stop feeling sorry for myself and see a chiropodist.

SUNDAY LUNCH

The wife said to me, "We've been invited to lunch by Auntie Elsie."
I said, "I can't go because on TV Manchester are playing Chelsea."
The wife said, "You can't disappoint the old dear.
It won't hurt you to go – it's only once a year."
"Can't you tell your auntie I'm not very well?"
"I know you don't want to go and auntie will know, I can tell.
Anyway, if I was to go by myself,
What excuse would I give old Aunt Else?"
I was thinking hard now to find some excuse.
I gave up in the end – well, what was the use?
So off we went to Sunday lunch with our relation.
I was certainly not looking forward to this – that's no exaggeration.
So off we went to Auntie's. We rang on the doorbell.
She answered the door – she was pleased, I could tell.
"Come in, come in. I've cooked a nice Sunday roast.
I know that's the lunch that all men like most."
We sat down to dine. Well, I don't know where to begin –
It just looked so dreadful when she brought the meal in.
The sprouts looked overcooked, all yellow and soggy;
The carrots were mushy and decidedly dodgy.
As for the roast spuds, I don't know where to begin –
You'd need a pair of nutcrackers to even get in.
Now, as for the roast beef – I don't mean to make fun –
It was cooked to a cinder, decidedly well done.
Then there was gravy looking very much like tar,
And the taste it was awful, like oil from a car.
Auntie was looking at me with a smile on her face.
I didn't have the heart to tell her I couldn't stand the taste.
I tried to be diplomatic, and even polite;
I tried to explain, I didn't have a big appetite.

Then there was afters – custard and a big apple pie.
I suppose I must eat some or at least give it a try.
The pie looked really well done, I could tell –
Not a bit like pastry, more like a tortoise shell.
The custard was lumpy, the pie it was cold;
I'd like to complain, but I wasn't that bold.
When lunchtime was over we had several cups of tea.
I could feel the whole concoction sloshing around in me.
With Aunt Elsie's cooking there were so many faults,
And my stomach was now doing all sorts of somersaults.
After much conversation, and being much far too polite,
We told Auntie it was time to be going and bade her goodnight.
On the way home the wife said, "Now, what about that?"
None too politely I said, "Not very much, as a matter of fact.
In fact," I said, "not seeming too rude,
Even dogs would turn up their nose at that kind of food.
You'd think that someone would tell her she can't cook.
Someone like you should buy her a recipe book."
The wife said, "You should be grateful for all that you had."
I said, "Leave it out! She'd even ruin a cold green salad."
She wouldn't talk to me for the rest of the way home,
But as we got to the door she let out a groan.
When she eventually emerged from the loo,
She said, "I'm sorry – I have to agree with you.
That meal was awful and we're invited for Christmas Day."
"You'll just have to tell her sorry, but we're going away."

CHILDHOOD

I often think and wonder why
I think of childhood with moistened eye.
But after pondering for a while,
Thinking thoughts that make me smile:
The icy patterns on windowpane,
Jack Frost has done his art again;
Cold winter's days I'd stay inside,
And I'd be quite satisfied
To play away for hours on end
With my imaginary friend.
We'd play at cowboys with a horse –
It would only be a chair, of course.
Baking days would be when
Mother made little gingerbread men.
Summer days that seemed so long,
And blackbirds sing their pretty song,
When washday bubbles filled the air –
Oh, what memories to share!
When soapy rainbow-coloured bubbles
Float away like childhood troubles!
And, after play days I remember this:
Mother's tender goodnight kiss.

SHAVING TIME

It's early morning and the alarm clock's ring.
I put out my hand to switch off that awful din.
I make my way to the bathroom to shave and shower.
Why do we do this at this unearthly hour?
Just think of the time we could save
If we didn't have to wash or shave.
I look in the mirror and just grimace –
Am I really the owner of that awful face?
Face so dark and full of multicoloured stubble.
If the razor's not sharp, I'm in real big trouble.
I start to shave with the aid of foam –
I've got to look smart when I leave from home.
Sideburns trimmed and hair combed neat,
Aftershave applied – must try to smell sweet.
Put on my clothes and just get dressed,
Try to look smart – well, I'll do my best.
No time for breakfast, I'm in too much hurry!
I'm running late, so off to work I scurry.
On arrival at work, I put on the kettle
Just to make tea, but there's no time to settle.
I'm about to sit down and the telephone rings.
That's when requests start and the workday begins.
I work all day because work we all must –
That's how we get a living and earn our crust.

THE SHED

Me and Mum went out one day,
Not too many streets away.
We're going out for Sunday tea;
We're going to Gran's, Mum and me.
We'll have nice sandwiches and some cakes –
I like everything my granny bakes.
Granddad saw us and said, "I found a stove,"
Smiling as if he had found some treasure trove.
"You're a hoarder," I heard my Gran say.
"You just won't throw anything away."
Gran said, "Come on in." We sat down to eat,
Granddad smiling, sitting in his special seat.
He went on and on about what he'd got
Down the garden in his special plot.
Granddad said he owned an old tin hat.
They both laughed and said, "Why do you want that?"
"It might come in handy – you never know."
"You should have thrown that out long ago.
Just take a look in his old tin trunk –
It's full of rubbish, just a load of junk."
"You'd be surprised!" I heard him mutter.
"Not everything I've got is clutter."
Then Gran smiled and I heard her say,
"Why don't you get down, dear – go outside and play.
But just you listen and mind what I said:
Just keep away from Granddad's old shed."
So as the grown-ups laughed and talked and talked,
I slid down from the table and away I walked.
I went to the shed and took a little peek,
And, because nobody was looking, inside I did sneak.
I scraped the cobwebs from my dirty face
And thought, 'This shed is a right disgrace.'

Although it had got a sign that said 'DO NOT ENTER',
I thought it was to me a real adventure.
Should I creep in further? Did I dare?
Perhaps there would be hidden treasure there.
But there were rusty nails and a great big saw –
I'd never seen one that big before.
Axes, choppers and an old billhook –
I just had to take a much closer look.
On seeing it – it was a very strange selection,
Odds and ends, a very weird collection,
Drills and chisels and other such curios –
I had never seen things quite like those.
Then I saw a row of tins on a shelf.
I just had to take a look to satisfy myself.
I'd never seen pots and tins quite like those.
I just had to have a closer look – a real good nose.
Then the peace and quiet was shattered
As the shelf collapsed and down it clattered.
One great big tin from the shelf
Spilled this sticky stuff all over myself.
"Come on out!" I heard Mother shout.
"Come on out or you'll get a clout."
I opened the door and as I appeared
I heard a gasp – I must have looked weird.
Poor old Gran went into a deep faint
When she saw me covered in bright-red paint.
She hit the ground with an awful thud –
I suppose she thought I was covered in blood.
My mum said, "Lord, you are a stupid kid!
Go on – just look at what you just did."
I was so ashamed I hid my face –
I was going home in deep disgrace.
But Gran put her arms round me, as all Grans do,
And said, "Never mind, dear – we still love you."

SPRING

When you walk down road or lane,
See how the trees are in leaf again.
Admire the beauty of nature's scene –
All the many different shades of green.
The wild parsley do our verges grace,
Remind us of delicate old-fashioned lace.
When hawthorn blooms and blackbirds sing,
Surely these things herald spring.
So take time to ponder at your leisure;
Think of this time and place to treasure.
Dispel the thoughts of winter gloom;
Think of warmer days and summer soon.

MIRROR, MIRROR

Mirror, mirror on the wall,
Is this the image of a fool?
Receding hairline and furrowed brow –
It seems the years have flown by somehow.
With eyebrows now thicker than my hairline,
I know that I am in sharp decline.
"It comes to us all," I hear you say,
But it didn't worry me yesterday.
I saw someone on the telly just like me,
Talking of how things used to be.
The swinging sixties – that's a laugh!
Then I looked at an old photograph.
I was quite smart in days gone by,
But that's all gone now and the reason why
Is that in good food I did indulge
And so developed this stomach bulge.
So please don't laugh, it's rather sad;
Just remember me as someone's dad.

NOT GOOD ENOUGH

I'd like to tell you of a brief romance I once had
Some years ago, I remember, when I was a lad.
She was a pretty girl, distinctly middle class.
I thought I'd try to chat her up, just for laughs.
I gave her the usual chat-up lines – you know the sort of stuff.
I think she sort of liked me, or perhaps she fancied a bit of rough.
We went out together a few times, one a special date,
Then she said she had something to ask that couldn't wait:
"You've been invited round to our house for Sunday tea."
I thought, 'Why would her mum and dad want to meet the likes of me?'
So on the appointed day I went to this select neighbourhood,
Dressed up in my best suit – I thought that would be good.
I knocked on the front door. The girlfriend said, "Won't you come in?"
Her parents stood just behind her looking as miserable as sin.
When introductions were over we all went and sat down,
Then the old man proceeded to look me up and down.
He studied me like something out of the cattle market,
And her mother made me feel as welcome
As a turd on the dining-room carpet.
She looked down her nose at me with deep disapproval –
I knew she would be happy with my immediate removal.
Then there was him: you know the sort, plum in his gob,
Never done any real work – well, not a physical job.
Then I went through it, the dreaded inquisition.
What was my aim in life? Where and what was my position?
"May I ask what prospects you've got, young man?"
"Me, I'm a labourer and I go to work in a beat-up old van."
Then came the call: "Shall we adjourn for tea?"
Conversation now over, I thought, 'That'll suit me.'
We sat down at the table set out with bone china.
It looked very impressive – sandwiches on plates – it couldn't be finer.

But on taking a second look it wasn't much of a spread.
I don't think we were supposed to eat food, but paper doilies instead.
When teatime was over her parents went into the kitchen,
Talking in lowered voices – I suppose so that we couldn't listen.
I could hear them in the kitchen, whispering in deep debate.
He said to her, "He's one of those oiks from the housing estate."
Me and the girlfriend sat on the sofa having a chat.
I said, "I'm sorry, but I can't put up with much more of that.
I think you're a lovely girl and a bit of a gem,
But when you get older will you be acting and thinking like them?
Because they wouldn't accept someone who didn't go to the right school,
They would always treat me as if I were a bit of a fool.
I don't think I'd ever be good enough for their daughter,
And, if we even tried, it would be like mixing oil and water."
So then we walked to the door and there we said goodbye.
I gave her a kiss on the cheek; she had a tear in her eye.
Now some people might think they're a different class,
But in truth it's all so much of a big farce
Because we all live in the same world that we share,
And we all live, walk, talk and breathe the same air.

LITTLE CHILDREN

I'm sure there can't be a much happier sound
Than the laughter of children in a playground.
So shame on those who would have them grow up too fast!
Let them grow naturally and let childhood last.
So let them play games that are secret, and pretend
That us adults have long forgotten or don't comprehend.
Don't burden them with worldly troubles and make them insecure.
Problems of life will come soon enough, that's for sure.
And it's always a simple but very pleasant thing
To hear the beautiful young voices of little children sing.
So surely it should be every child's perfect right
To go to bed in comfort and sleep safe at night
And dream away contentedly of happy and pleasant things,
And so look forward to tomorrow and what
New adventure a new day brings.

MOTHER AND DAUGHTER

It was just the other evening I was sitting with my eyes closed;
The wife and daughter were talking –
They thought I wasn't listening, I suppose.
The daughter was asking her mother for some advice
About her latest boyfriend, who she thought was very nice.
She said, "He's very handsome and he's so polite,
And he really flatters me when he kisses me goodnight.
I think he's going to ask me to set up home with him."
The wife said, "I should be very careful – it may be just a whim.
I know he may be very handsome, he's also very young,
But the boys you should be wary of are those with the silver tongue.
Now, I don't want to put you off or raise any fears,
Think what he's going to be like in just a few years.
Compare him to his father – that's the best thing you can do –
Because that's what he's going to be like, I am telling you.
But as for men in general, if you want to compare,
Look at the state of your father asleep in that old chair.
Look at him sound asleep there with his great beer belly!
Most of them are all hairy and their feet are rather smelly.
Men are dirty creatures and they make such a mess,
And even if you try to change them, you won't have much success.
Now take the other night: he crept home so late,
And, when I started moaning, his excuse was he'd met a mate.
He'd been down the pub, that was true, I could tell –
The way he staggered in and by the awful smell.
Another thing is, when they're late home, sometimes for hours,
You know they've been up to something when they bring you flowers.
Now, I don't want to deter you from becoming a partner or a wife,
But just think very carefully before you commit yourself for life.
Your dad's like that – a great fat useless lump."
That's when I got up, slammed the door and went to bed with the hump.

CHEEKY!

Mother said, "You can come to town with me today on a shopping trip.
I can't trust you here alone – you give the neighbours too much lip.
I know when I go out you usually go round your Auntie Sue's,
But since she had you last time – you played her up – she just refused.
I don't know how you upset her, but, whatever you said or did,
My sister said she's never known such a rude and cheeky kid."
So as we left by our front door, I saw the next-door neighbour.
I don't know what it means, but my dad reckons she's a 'raver'.
All I said was, "I saw you first thing this morning.
When you opened your front door, you were still yawning.
You spoke to the milkman and asked him in for a cup of tea.
Do you know him well, or did you just want company?"
"If it's anything to do with you, young man, he's my younger brother.
Just mind your own business! He's certainly not my lover."
Mum said I was an embarrassment and I had too much to say,
And, before she could clip me round the ear, I ducked out the way.
We saw our other neighbour on our way back from town.
Mum said, "Now you just behave yourself – don't act the clown."
I called out, "Hi. How are you? How are you doing, Mr Brown?
You make me laugh when you laugh, 'cause your belly jumps up and down."
My mum said, "I knew your mouth would get you in trouble."
She grabbed my ear and marched me quickly home at the double.
Now I've been sent to bed early for having too much cheek –
Mum said I was very rude to the people down our street.
And now it's time to contemplate as I walk up the stair,
And, as I think things over, I don't really care.
I can now go to my room and take a real good look,
And read, and have a laugh at those funny characters in my comic book.

MUM

You only ever have one mum,
And I've got a very special one.
When I was young and just a kid
I remember all the special things she did,
Like keep me clean and wash my clothes,
Comb my hair and even wipe my runny nose.
When I did fret when others tease,
Mum would put my worried mind at ease.
There were many times that I recall
She would pick me up if I should fall.
She would brush me down and clean the dirt,
And tenderly she would heal the hurt.
If I was sick or in poor health,
Mum would tend me, never thinking of herself.
So now I've grown up and got a little wiser,
I won't forget Mum, my chief advisor.
The worldly things that give you joy and hope,
The good advice mums give you, so you can cope –
With all the problems, big or small,
Mum taught me how to deal with them all.
So thank you to a dear and special mum –
You surely are a very special one.

THE INTERVIEW

I've come to this establishment for a job interview.
Some others have as well – there are quite a few.
I've put on a suit, cleaned my shoes and worn a tie;
I need this job badly so my hardest I will try –
Not like that other chap, who's sitting over there
In old tattered jeans, tee shirt and really unkempt hair.
I don't think coming like that creates a good impression –
Perhaps he doesn't want the job and prefers some other profession.
There's another chap waiting as well. He looks a little sick,
And if he bites his nails much more they'll be down to the quick.
Then there's this other bloke, he's getting on everyone's nerves,
Telling all the rest of us we're only there as first reserves.
"We might as well all go home," said the nail-biter.
I said, "Take no notice of him; he's just a bragging blighter.
That's what he wants – a clear run for the one position.
If we all leave now, he's got no opposition."
Just then this lady took him away for his interview.
The room went deadly quiet, but it was nice and peaceful too.
Twenty minutes later I was shown the interview-room door.
I thought, 'Just relax and answer the questions; you've done this before.'
There were three people there to conduct the interviews.
I suppose it's very difficult knowing which candidate to choose.
They said, "Come in and sit down. We'll try to put you at ease.
We've got a few questions for you to answer, if you could, please.'

They asked me about my home life and have I any hobbies,
And if I was in work right now what my present job is.
I explained I worked in a supermarket stacking shelves at night,
And having to sleep all through the day doesn't feel quite right.
"I really need a day job for a better social life,
And I would really like to see much more of the kids and wife."
"That's all very well," they said, "but what can you offer us?"
I replied, "Hard work and loyalty, good timekeeping and trust.
I've never had much sick time – I'm lucky in that way.
It seems I'm blowing my own trumpet, so there's not much more to say."
They then all thanked me for attending the interview,
And said that they would be in touch in a day or two.
I think I might have got this job – that's what I told the wife.
I really hope I have because that would complete my life.

FLIES

Just when I thought I would have a lay in bed,
This blasted fly started buzzing round my head.
Why doesn't it clear off and irritate someone else instead?
"Why don't you stop fidgeting?" – that's what the wife said.
"It's this damn fly," I said. "Now it's landed on my nose.
I suppose I'd better get up and put on some clothes."
As fast as I could, because it was still buzzing round me,
I covered the private and confidential parts of my anatomy.
I chased the fly round the room with a rolled-up newspaper,
Vowing I'd kill it – I'd had enough of its caper.
The wife said, "Don't kill it, for goodness' sake.
If you do, you'll have a dozen more come to its wake."
I splattered it on the wall. I thought, 'That's end of game.'
I should have known better – half a dozen more,
In the window they came.
"I told you," the wife said, "you silly old fool."
Don't you just hate it when they're a right know-all!

FALSE TEETH

The road gang I worked with were a very mixed bunch.
We had many a laugh whilst having our lunch.
But there was this old boy that made the tea –
He had bad habits, things that you don't do in company.
One day when lunch was about halfway through
We could all see what he was going to do.
The foreman shouted a bit too late,
Because Alf had taken out his top plate.
Before the foreman had even moved his lips,
Alf had started to dig out the tomato pips.
"Put your choppers back in!" came the shout.
Too late! By now he'd taken the bottom plate out.
The foreman said, "Now, look here, Alf –
If you want to do that, sit by yourself.
It's more than rude, it's downright crude,
Taking your teeth out while others are eating their food."
Now Alf, being an awkward old cuss,
Started moaning and making a lot of fuss.
He said, "When you get older and have false teeth
You'll be glad to take them out for a bit of relief."
"Look – we think it's bad manners. That's enough said.
Just do as you're asked and put them back in your head."
Alf did as he was asked, after having his say,
But he moaned and sulked for the rest of the day.

SNOBS?

The people over there on the new estate
Think that us on this side of the road are second rate.
Well, I think the new arrivals and people like those
That think they're so perfect get right up my nose.
The interlopers have taken over the cricket team and the tennis club;
They've even got the gall to try to take over our pub.
Well, I've got news for them if they did but know it:
We're just as good as them, but we just don't show it.
We may ride around in our old second-hand cars,
But at least we own them and we can say they're ours.
There's no finance company that's likely to snatch them back.
They're not new or good enough and that's a simple fact.
Now I'm not envious, jealous or even aggrieved;
I'd just like to explain, that lot there are just a different breed.
There's the geezer from number twenty-five,
Has a brand new BMW parked in his drive.
It's never moved one inch from the day it arrived.
I suppose he's trying to impress all the snobby neighbours,
But just standing there it's not doing anyone any favours.
Then there's the fella who rides the moped. He looks a proper charlie.
The way he sits astride it, he treats it like a Harley.
He rides it to the station to catch the London train,
And then in the evening he rides it back again.
He's some sort of salesman in a West End store,
But the way he brags about it, he's a right know-all bore.
Then there's the bloke with the orange tan –
Makes out he holidays Continental,
But everyone knows he gets his tan on a sunbed lying horizontal.

And what about the strange couple that live over there?
Both of them used to have pure snow-white hair.
But they've never been quite the same since
They have had a matching blue hair rinse.
And now I'm sure they've gone off their noodle,
Because they've even blue-rinsed their pet poodle.
And so, you see, it's going to take time for the city folk
To adjust to country life and not just be a joke.

BUMP START

I got into my car in the morning when it was still quite dark.
I turned the key in the ignition, but the engine wouldn't start.
I then got out from the car and gave the wheel a good old kick,
Thinking, 'I need this in the morning! It's enough to make you sick!'
My neighbour, who was standing there, said, "There's no need to panic."
He's a really helpful guy and quite a good mechanic.
He said, "Kicking the car won't help you; that won't make it go!
All you'll succeed in doing is to hurt your flippin' toe!
I think it's the battery – I'm quite sure of that.
The way the engine's firing sounds like the battery's flat.
I think we can get it started, so don't you give up hope.
We'll push it just along the road and bump-start it down the slope."
Another good neighbour came along, by the name of Carter,
Said, "I'll help you push the car and see if we can start her."
Now as we pushed the car along the road, along came Mr Wise.
He said, "What's the matter? Won't it start?"
"Nah, we push cars just for exercise!"
Pushing the car and steering, I can hear my heart.
All we can hope for now is a first-time start!
Now jump in the car, turn the key, then let out the clutch,
Foot on the throttle, plenty of revs, but not too much.
We got the motor started and to work I'm on my way.
All I can say is, "Thank you, guys. Hip hip hooray!"
Now I really must remember, when I get home tonight
I must go round and thank my neighbours – that would only be polite!

FRED

I still love my old teddy bear.
He's only got one eye, but I don't care.
There's one ear missing and he's nearly bald,
But everyone knows what my teddy bear is called.
Mummy says he's threadbare, so his name is Fred,
But I don't care what his name is when I take him up to bed.
When it comes to bedtime and I go to bed at night,
I snuggle down under the covers and hug old Fred real tight.
If me and my teddy bear were separated or parted,
I'm sure I would cry myself to sleep really broken-hearted,
Because there is no other toy I would like instead.
He is really cuddly, my lovely Mr Fred.

DON'T EAT BETWEEN MEALS

When I go round to Granny's on my way home from school,
I know that I shouldn't, but I break the golden rule.
When I walk through the doorway, Gran says, "What's the matter?"
I pull a face and give her a right load of old patter.
"Gran, I'm really starving." That was not quite the truth;
And If my mum had heard it, she would hit the roof,
Because Mum says I shouldn't eat between meals.
But I feel so hungry – that's how my stomach feels.
"Don't they feed you at that school? Didn't you have dinner?
I must say you do look peaky, and a little thinner.
Are you sure you're really hungry?" I said, "Yes, I am."
She said, "If you're that hungry, I'll do you bread and jam.
Or go into the kitchen and look up on the shelf –
There you'll find the biscuit tin. Go and help yourself.
What's the matter? Can't you find it? Can't you find the tin?"
"Yeah, I found that all right, but I can't find one with chocolate in."
"Now I think you're getting a bit saucy, that's what you are."
I thought I might have pushed my luck a little bit too far.
"I think I'd better be off home now. Mum will wonder where I am."
So I chucked my kitbag round my shoulder and said goodbye to Gran.
I got home and sat down to my meal.
After a few mouthfuls I was stuffed.
Mother said, "That's it! I'm fed up. I've really had enough.
I suppose you've been round your gran's again, eating between meals.
If you had to prepare the dinner, you'd know how it feels.
It makes me really angry, and I get bloomin' mad,
But I suppose it won't go to waste – it'll just mean more for Dad."

AUNTIE DOT

Mum and Dad and me went round to see my Auntie Dot.
She's a very lovely lady, but she don't half talk a lot.
We knocked the door; she answered it and said, "Come on in."
She said, "Nice to see you. It's been some time. Where have you all been?
Sit yourselves down. I'll put the kettle on and make some tea."
She went to the kitchen, still talking, yakking on constantly.
She was going on now about some old boy's operation.
The way she put it you'd think it was a celebration.
Now Auntie's voice is quite distinct, and is very loud.
You could pick it out in any really noisy crowd.
Sitting down with us now, she said, "It's time for a chat."
I thought to myself, 'I don't know too much about that!
The way that you go on and on – now, what's the phrase? –
No one else is going to get a word in edgeways!'
I had a very hard job to stifle and suppress a yawn,
As she talked about things that happened before I was born.
I saw on my dad's face a look of real consternation,
And I could see he was getting bored with this one-sided conversation.
After about two hours of this incessant constant repetition,
And without not too much interruption or competition,
It was just about then Dad got up and said in a voice quite distinct,
"It's time for us to be getting back home, I think."
Auntie said, "Is it that time? Oh dear! Must you really go?
It's been so nice and I have enjoyed our conversation so."
On the way home Dad said, "Good grief! For Heaven's sake!
She never stops! How that woman's jaws must ache!
In fact, when she goes to bed and takes out her false teeth
And puts them in a glass of water they must let out a sigh of relief!"

WE NEED A ROTA

I got up quite early this morning, I must say,
Trying to get to the bathroom first – not like yesterday.
I crept to the bathroom whilst no one was stirring.
We don't want yesterday's ruckus reoccurring!
But all my best efforts were all in vain:
My teenage daughter had beaten me yet again.
"Hurry up in there!" I shouted through the door.
"I've complained and told you so many times before!
I need to get in the bathroom to shave and to shower.
You know I have to be at work in less than an hour!
Will you hurry up and come out of there?"
"I'll try not to be too long – I'm washing my hair."
Right about now – it was as I had feared –
The wife in the bedroom doorway appeared.
"Will you keep the noise down? What's all the fuss?
You didn't have to start shouting and wake up the rest of us!
Will you please keep quiet and keep down the noise!
If you both keep it up, you're going to wake up the boys!"
I thought, 'That's all I need first thing in the morning –
Her standing there nagging whilst she is still yawning!'
At last her ladyship emerged, said smugly, "Are you satisfied?"
"I would be if you didn't take so blinking long!" I replied.
I thought, 'Now it's my turn.' Or so it would seem –
But I couldn't see anything with a room full of steam!
So I wiped off the mirror and I started to sing –
I don't know why, because I couldn't see a thing.
I got out my razor and proceeded to shave.
Now, that was plain stupid, trying to be brave.
On my way to work I thought, 'I must look a disgrace
With all the bits of tissue covering the cuts on my face.'
As I was going along, thinking and driving the motor,
I thought, 'The answer to this problem is to work out a rota!'

DRESSING UP

All little girls like dressing up, that's a well-known fact,
So do you remember a few years ago when you did just that?
You'd walk up and down the hallway in your mummy's clothes,
Looking quite proud of yourself putting on junior fashion shows.
Skirts hitched high and gathered around your little waist,
With head held high still up and down and round and round you paced.
Although the clothes they didn't fit, you still looked so very proud;
Clumping up and down in high-heeled shoes, it was rather loud.
It must have hurt your feet, let alone your toes,
Trying to walk in those grown-ups' fashionable stilettos.
And what about the lipstick? It was so very bright red.
You didn't put it on your lips, but right round your mouth instead.
Another time you tried Mum's nail varnish and wondered how she could tell.
It never even occurred to you that she went by the smell.
But when you went to the wardrobe and tried on Mother's bra,
I think you were told quite firmly you had gone too far.
This is all part of growing up; it's a female preserve.
Every girl should be allowed to dress up – it's called the learning curve.
But on this very special day we're so full of pride
Because today Mummy's little angel is the blushing bride.

HANDBAGS AND SHOES

My wife's got a collection of handbags and shoes.
When we go out she doesn't know which ones to choose.
When packing the cases for our holiday last year,
She laid out the shoes and said, "What do you think, dear?"
"I don't know," I said, "but don't take too many."
"Huh – if you had your way, I wouldn't take any!
I need at least two pairs; I need black and brown –
They're normal colours of shoes for around town.
I'll need shoes for the beach with open toes;
I'll need those fashionable ones for going to shows.
I think I'll take the purple ones – they're my favourite –
Also the bright-blue ones, that's if they still fit!"
Now, if my reckoning is correct, that's six pairs already.
I just hope with the other clothing she's taking it steady.
And now for the handbags: "I'll need at least three.
What do you think, dear?" "It's no good asking me!"
"I'll take one black, one brown and one coloured buff.
Should I take four or will three be enough?"
When packing the cases with skirts, dresses and other clothes,
There wasn't much room for my stuff –
But it doesn't matter, I suppose.
When loading the car with the help of my son,
He said, "Blimey, Dad, these cases must weigh a ton!"
Now my ideal holiday is some backwoods retreat,
But the wife's idea is some busy shopping street.

We'll walk up and down the street no matter the weather,
Looking for shoes and handbags made of real leather.
Most other shops we just pass on by,
But shoes or handbags we give it a try.
"Just look at those shoes in the window!"
Two seconds later without hesitation in the shop we go.
I hate to admit it, but it's become a tradition
To come back off our holiday with at least one addition.
This year it was two pairs of shoes and a handbag,
But if I'm honest, I should be really glad.
It could easily be so much more expensive things,
Like necklaces, bracelets or gold and diamond rings!

OUR ANNIVERSARY

Tomorrow is the anniversary of our wedding day,
And I really must do my best to find a card to say
How much I really love you, and with words sincere,
To cherish and to comfort and truly love you, dear.
A present I must find to prove I really care,
And perhaps to show the world all the love we share.
Perhaps I'll buy you chocolates – fancy, special, Continental –
Or silk or satin clothing, luxury-type, Oriental.
But if I were to ask you, I'm sure you'd smile and say,
"You know I love flowers and I'd rather have a nice bouquet."

MY NEW WELLIES

It's been raining outside, but I don't give two hoots,
'Cause I'm lucky my mum's bought me a pair of wellington boots.
My mummy said, "Let's go for a walk down the lane.
If we put our coats on, it won't matter about the rain."
I can try out my wellies and see if they leak;
I've been hoping to try them out all of this week.
Running about, now rushing, darting and dashing,
In all the puddles I could find I was splashing.
'Coo – look right there! It's a huge great big one.
I wonder if I could jump right in it and splash my mum.'
I held my breath and took a great big leap,
But I didn't realise it was going to be quite deep.
That's when my mum seemed to go quite berserk.
She shouted at me and said, "Now look at my skirt!"
I thought she would laugh, but I might as well be joking
Because all our clothes were thoroughly wet through and soaking.
She said, "Come here right now! Are you satisfied?"
That's when I felt sorry, rubbed my eyes and nearly cried.
We'll have to go back home now and go back inside;
We'll have to wait and make sure our clothes have all dried.
Now that we're home, I'll have to stay in all day.
Even if the sun shines, I won't be able to go out and play.
I'll just lie on the carpet, lie on my belly,
With my head in my hands, just watching the telly!

THE OPEN FIRE

I'm sure most youngsters would have a laugh
If they saw me sweeping ashes from the hearth,
Because most homes now have central heating,
And for warmth and cleanliness it takes some beating.
Not for them taking out ashes and getting in coal!
All they do is turn on a thermostat control.
They don't have a fireplace – well, that's their decision.
The focal point of their home is the television.
I'm afraid to say, it's still my desire
On winter's nights to warm my backside by the fire,
To sit and watch the coals or logs really glow
And forget about the wind, rain or snow.
Recently we had our friends come to visit,
And can you guess where they chose to sit?
That's right – they said they can really feel the heat,
A nice coal or log fire is really hard to beat.
And as we sat and talked of things, we reminisced
Of families and friends and other things we missed.
There's nothing better than sitting by the fire at night,
Talking with friends and putting the world to right.
Anyway, I'd need far too much nagging and coercion
To agree to having an electric or gas conversion.
The different ways of heating can be very scientific,
But to me an open fire will always be terrific.
So now I'll bank up the fire, as that's enough said.
I've said my little piece, so I'm going up to bed.

BAD HABITS

It was quite a few years ago, when I was a kid,
Mum would give us good advice on everything we did.
Manners they were everything – she couldn't stand bad habits.
You didn't misbehave yourself – Mother would not have it.
She would say, "No talking with your mouth full!
It's really rather rude"
And "Sit up straight at the table – get on and eat your food."
And she would say, "Don't scratch like that, dear – not in company.
If you carry on scratching, they'll think you've got a flea."
I wonder what she would think now of the way that some behave.
I'm sure if she could see it now, she'd be turning in her grave.
She also said to me one day, "Don't play with those load of scruffs –
The ones from down the road with stiff and silver cuffs."
I wonder what she would make of it with people like those
Who stand right in the open and blatantly pick their nose.
There was this bloke I know – ladies, you wouldn't want to watch –
He'd be right in the open and stand and scratch his crotch.
Now, I know we've all got bad habits, but the ones that annoy me
Are people that smack their chops when eating,
And ones that slurp their tea.

THE BEST MAN'S SPEECH

Our wedding plans and the big day was all set,
So I thought to myself about the best man I would get.
I asked my best mate to be best man at our wedding,
But on the day would he make a speech I was dreading?
I had a really good stag night, the party was good –
It was a really good way to end my bachelorhood.
After the church service we went to the reception.
All the guests were well seated without exception.
When everyone was settled, my mate got up. He was swaying.
You couldn't understand or make out a word he was saying.
He just stood there and started muttering something half-hearted.
Oh dear! And that's when the barracking started.
Then my old man started with the slow handclap
And shouted out loud, "We want a good speech, old chap."
Someone else: "You had enough to say for yourself last night,
When you'd had too much to drink and were more than half tight!
Give him a whisky and make it a very large one.
That should get him started – it'll help loosen his tongue!"
Someone gave him a large drink. He swallowed it down.
He looked at me; I pulled a face and gave him a frown.
Our best man then rapped on the top table
And said, "I'll make the proposals of thanks if I'm able,
But first raise your glasses to the bride and the groom.
We all wish you good luck – everyone in the room.
Secondly, may I thank the bridesmaids for a job really well done.
We'd like to thank them all, each and every one.
I could tell by now he'd got in his stride,
And thought to myself, 'There goes my pride!
Why did they have to get him that well oiled?
Now my reputation is really going to be soiled.'

He said, "I never thought my very good friend here
Would ever make it to a marriage career.
I didn't think he'd give up the football and the booze;
We never thought it was a path that he'd choose.
Chatting up all the girls was his way of life;
We never thought he'd settle down with a wife.
I could tell you even more things about him –
About when he stripped off starkers and went for a swim.
In the village pond it was, honest, I swear.
When he got out, he ran down the street completely bare.
That's why we call Will [that's me] Willie Wonker –
Because when he was running you could see his old plonker."
My new mother-in-law, with tears in her eyes,
Said to my new wife, "I'm sure he's telling lies!"
Mother-in-law's hat on her head was askew –
By this time of the proceedings she'd had quite a few!
Now his expression had changed, and his words were all slurred.
He said, "I can tell you about many more things that occurred.
Don't look so shocked now – we know how you feel.
Most of you only came for free booze and a meal."
Old Aunt Bessie, I could see, was in a state of real shock.
Her face was so red it nearly matched her old frock.
But Uncle Charlie you could see didn't care.
He was laughing so much he nearly fell off his chair.
The whole speech was over when he slipped to the floor.
I thought, 'Thank goodness for that! I couldn't take any more!'
We all agreed it was best to let him lie there and sleep –
That was the best way for other dark secrets to keep.
Everyone agreed the rest of the evening went with a swing.
As for the best man, in the morning he won't remember a thing.
I whispered to my new wife, "We'll slip away real soon.
I think it's time we left for our honeymoon."

DIESEL

When I was younger and in my prime
I did roadworks for a living for quite a time.
Now this chap that I'm going to tell you about
Is quite a character, of that there's no doubt.
When I first started I was a bit dim –
I couldn't understand why nobody wanted to work with him.
Everybody else chuckled and said I was brave
When I volunteered to work with Diesel Dave.
"Why do you call him that?" I just had to say.
They laughed and said, "You'll find out by the end of the day."
Dave asked the foreman, "Shall I fuel up the machines?"
He grinned and said, "You two go ahead, by all means."
So, can in hand, the dumper was first on the list,
But when Dave poured the gas oil out, he well and truly missed.
Red diesel or gas oil – whatever you may call it –
Went all over Dave's trousers. What a stupid twit!
"That's next," said Dave, pointing to the air compressor.
He marched over to it like some roadworks professor.
I said, "When you're pouring it, take it slow.
Remember a quart into a pint pot won't go."
He looked at me and said, "I don't need your advice.
I've done this job before more than once or twice."
But still he overfilled the brand-new machine.
I thought, 'I'll keep my mouth shut – don't want to cause a scene.'

He said, "We'll do the tractor next. I'll climb up on it,"
And then he started filling it up, standing on the bonnet.
Then he slipped and let the whole diesel can go.
What a mess! Diesel oil over the tractor, all over the show!
He soaked himself in gas oil; he said he didn't care.
I said, "Well, I blinkin' do. You got it over me – it's even in my hair."
I said, "Why don't you use a funnel, or even a pump?"
He said, "All right, mate, you don't have to get the hump."
I said, "Instead of rushing into things, why don't you stop and think?
Then we wouldn't have to work in clothes that really stink."
The other blokes had stopped working, just to see the show.
I said, "He likes the smell of diesel."
They said, "Tell us somethin' we don't know."
They laughed and said, "That's why we call him Diesel Dave.
We reckon he uses it as bubble bath when he has a bathe,
And when he goes out at night he uses it as aftershave."
If ever a man earned his nickname, Dave certainly did.
I won't get near him when he's got diesel – not for 100 quid.

TOO MUCH INFORMATION

The Freedom of Information Act
Is a law I am sure most people would back,
But I thought it came in to unearth spies
And to clear up the mess caused by political lies –
Not to spy on people who lead everyday lives
Or to report on things that go on between husbands and wives.
If that's what they want, I could do them a favour:
We could recruit thousands of people like my old next-door neighbour.
If she was in the neighbourhood watch, it's my belief
They would certainly have to make her colonel-in-chief.
When I staggered home from the pub late at night,
I knew she'd be there behind the curtains just out of sight.
As I walked down the path I could see the curtains twitch,
And I know I'm being spied on by that nosey old bitch.
Sometimes I thought it would've been quite a hoot
To give the nosey cow a two-fingered salute.
She always knew our business – I don't know how.
She was just one of those people: a right nosey cow.
Why do people like that want to know our affairs?
Are our lives much more interesting than theirs?
Now, for most of my life, and I can't explain why,
I have been what's usually called camera-shy.
I lead a quiet life for most of the while;
I keep my head down and keep a low profile.

On going to town with people around there was a bit of confusion.
Then I could see what bothered me –
The chap who was the cause of intrusion.
Right there he did stand, flash camera in hand,
And then came the question I was dreading:
"Take your photograph, sir?" "No, thank you, mate!
You're already too late – I had it done at my wedding."
Further along down the street who should I meet?
It was a lady doing a survey.
I tried to dodge by, but, no matter how hard I did try,
She managed to stand in my way.
Just about then, with clipboard and pen,
She said, "Just a few questions, sir, about things you prefer."
I made up my mind then, and couldn't pretend,
And asked why it concerned her.
I said, "I think you should know that some time ago
I came to this important decision:
I simply resolved to not get involved
With politics, scandal or religion."
So what we have learned is we should be concerned
Because someone is looking at us.
So I'll be quiet now and manage somehow
Not to cause too much fuss.

SHADOWS

With lights turned out and day is done,
The ghostly shadows have their fun.
Is that the way that shadows fall?
Or is there someone in the hall?
Look over by the stair –
I'm sure there's something lurking there.
I thought I heard somebody speak,
But it was only the floorboards' creak.
Look under the bed, in cupboard too –
What a stupid thing to do!
Too much thought and hesitation –
They could thwart the investigation.
Are there ghosts? Don't be absurd!
Too many stupid stories you have heard.
Go to bed and go to sleep.
Night-time is when shadows creep.
Night's for you to dream away;
Tomorrow is another day.

BIG-HEAD

As we go through life we've often heard it said,
"No one likes a know-it-all; no one likes a big-head" –
The ones that have an opinion on everything you do,
But when it comes down to it they haven't got a clue.
I don't really know what makes this type of person tick;
They seem to treat all the rest of us as if we're really thick.
Where do they get their ideas?
From where do they get their knowledge?
Certainly not from any school I went to and certainly not from college!
But they seem to get on well in life, and it seems so unjust
Because when it comes down to it they're the ones you cannot trust.
This chap, he came to work with us.
We thought he was the boss's favourite.
You know the type: a right big-headed know-it-all,
A right big-headed twit.
It nearly got to crisis point just the other day
When Big-Head put his foot in it because he had to have his say.
We were talking about wages – what a subject to discuss! –
When the boss looked in and said to him, "You should be paying us."
I was talking to the rest of them by way of conversation
About going out for the evening with a very close relation.
I said, "I went out for a meal last night and had a glass of wine."
"So did I," he stated. "I bet yours was not as good as mine."
Not to be outdone, I said, "I finished the whole bottle."
"So did I," he said. I muttered, "I know someone I'd like to throttle."
So it's a feeling that we all know, and often should be stated:
Take no notice of the big-heads in life or the self-opinionated.